BRICK MASONS ON THE JOB

BY AMY C. REA

MOMENTUM

childsworld.com

Published by The Child's World®
1980 Lookout Drive • Mankato, MN 56003-1705
800-599-READ • www.childsworld.com

Content Consultant: David L. Pryes, Masonry
Instructor, Northeast Wisconsin Technical College

Photographs ©: Shutterstock Images, cover, 1, 8,
18, 20; Dmitry Kalinovsky/Shutterstock Images,
5; iStockphoto, 6, 21, 23, 26, 28; Alexandre
Zveiger/Shutterstock Images, 9; Shcherbakov
Ilya/Shutterstock Images, 11; Air Images/
Shutterstock Images, 12; Monkey Business
Images/Shutterstock Images, 14; Julieann Birch/
iStockphoto, 15; Ozgur Coskun/Shutterstock
Images, 17; Yuri Arcurs/iStockphoto, 24; JPL
Designs/iStockphoto, 27

ISBN 9781503835542
LCCN 2019943068

Printed in the United States of America

CONTENTS

MOMENTUM

FAST FACTS

What's the Job?

► Brick masons lay and bind bricks together. Bricks are used to build walls, bridges, and other structures.

► Most masons are trained through **apprenticeships**. An apprenticeship can take three or four years. Apprentices are paid while they train on the job.

► Most masons work outdoors, even in bad weather. Most masons work full time.

Important Stats

► In 2018, the U.S. government estimated that 63,930 people worked as brick and block masons.

► Between 2016 and 2026, the demand for masons is expected to grow by 12 percent.

► In 2018, brick and block masons made an average yearly salary of $54,430.

**Brick masons usually kneel or stand for long periods ►
of time. They also have to lift heavy objects.**

CHAPTER ONE

THE BEGINNING OF A STADIUM

Jared looked at the steel beams in front of him. The beams reached high above his head. He could see the blue sky through them. There were people wearing yellow hard hats and safety glasses everywhere. Far overhead, a tall crane slowly lowered large pieces of building materials. Jared was looking at a brand-new football stadium under construction.

Jared had done many brick-laying jobs in the past. He worked on construction sites for apartment buildings and large stores. He also worked on projects to fix up historic buildings. Every project was different, which made Jared's work interesting. But this was the first time he would work on a stadium. The stadium would be the new home for a football team. He couldn't wait for the day when he could take his family to see the team play there.

◄ Stadiums can take years to build.

▲ **Brick buildings need to be maintained.
Brick masons can do repair jobs.**

Then, Jared could tell them about how he helped build the large structure.

He could also tell them how brick can help a building be more energy **efficient**. He could explain how brick is more sound resistant than other materials. That meant the roars of people cheering inside the stadium would not spill outside as easily. Jared could tell his kids to cheer as loudly as they liked.

But Jared knew that day would be many months away. Building a stadium takes lots of time. Stadiums are much larger than normal houses or stores. Jared was part of a huge team.

▲ **Brick is a good material to build with. One reason is because bricks last for a long time.**

The team of construction workers had many tasks to complete before the first football game could be played at the stadium.

Jared saw his boss, Dan, and waved at him. Dan was standing on a wide piece of concrete flooring. There were large steel beams making a sort of ceiling over Dan's head. Dan was looking at a set of **blueprints**. Jared joined him and looked at the activity all around them. Dan told him this spot would be one of the stadium's **concession** areas. Someday, people would buy hot dogs, popcorn, and other foods there.

There were shouts from workers all around them. Jared leaned closer to Dan to hear what he was saying. Dan pointed at the blueprint. He showed Jared where the brick wall would be built.

Jared heard the low rumble of a heavy truck behind him. The large truck slowly drove into the space behind the concrete floor. It had a trailer hooked to the back of it. On that trailer was a bright red machine called a **hydraulic** mixer. He would use it to mix the **mortar** that would act as glue to hold the bricks together. Jared remembered his dad telling him about mixing mortar by hand many years ago. It was much easier and more efficient to have a machine.

Dan and Jared studied the blueprints. Then, Dan helped Jared check the measurements for where the first wall would go. Nearby, there was a big stack of bricks wrapped in plastic. As soon as the first batch of mortar was ready, Jared could start.

Mortar is a mixture of cement, water, lime, and sand. ►

CHAPTER TWO

EDUCATION

Lauren stepped out of her car and into a busy parking lot. Before her was a large technical school. Students walked in and out of the school through propped-open glass doors surrounded by brick. Lauren took a deep breath. Today was her first day of classes to learn how to become a brick mason.

Lauren's father owned a construction company. She had spent the summer watching his crews as they worked. Under the hot sun, Lauren watched brick masons lift, move, and lay bricks to make all kinds of structures. She saw walls built from bricks, along with garden paths, sidewalks, and driveways. Lauren got to see brick patios and firepits built in people's backyards.

One day, her father took her to watch construction on a large store. The front of the store was decorated with brick. Lauren was amazed at how much of the material was needed.

◀ **Trade school programs will teach students masonry skills, such as laying bricks and building walls.**

▲ **Learning from skilled teachers can prepare students for the job.**

Lauren liked the idea of working with her hands. She wanted to build things, too.

The technical college was bursting with activity. The college had many courses for brick masons, and Lauren wanted to learn as much as possible. She had always liked science and math. These would be good skills to have as a brick mason. Math was important to make measurements on the job. Science was important for understanding how building worked. Lauren also enjoyed working outdoors. That was important because most masons work on projects outside.

▲ **Hands-on experience is a great way
for people to learn new skills.**

Lauren pulled her phone out of her backpack and looked
up her class schedule. Her first class was called Basic Masonry
Skills. The class description sounded interesting. It said she
would learn how to mix mortar. Then, she would learn different
ways of laying brick. The methods depended on the type of
project. Lauren knew that at the technical school, she would learn
how to read masonry diagrams and blueprints. She would also
learn about the power tools used in masonry.

Lauren found and walked into the brightly lit classroom where her course would be held. Her classmates were mostly men. They talked with one another as they found seats. Lauren gripped her new notebook and slid into an empty desk. She thought about her future as a brick mason. Lauren wondered what it would be like to have her own brick mason company someday. She knew before that day could come, she would need lots of on-the-job experience. Lauren wanted to learn different kinds of brick masonry work. She thought that she could try several different projects. Work could be done on the outside walls of buildings. Those buildings could be small or very big. Brick could also be used in driveways and walkways. It could be used to build a fireplace and chimney. Patios, fences, and fountains could be made of brick. Later, if Lauren liked one type of project, she could specialize in it. That meant she would mostly do one or two kinds of brick work.

The class quieted down as their teacher walked through the door. Lauren opened her notebook to a fresh white page. She was ready to learn everything she needed about the trade job.

Brick patios can be designed in many different ways. ▶

CHAPTER THREE

TRAINING

L ogan put his hand above his eyes to shade them from the sun as he looked at a white house with the bottom half of the siding torn off. Nearby, red bricks were stacked together and wrapped tightly in plastic.

Logan was on his first work assignment as an apprentice. He recently became an apprentice to the local bricklayers union. The union was a professional group. It existed to help protect workers. It also worked on training new masons. Logan would spend between three and four years learning the trade. He would study brick laying in a classroom at a local technical college. He would also get to practice what he learned at real job sites while earning money. Logan had taken beginning masonry classes and had learned a lot. He figured out how to read blueprints.

◄ **Brick masons need to pay careful attention when stacking bricks together.**

▲ **When stacking bricks, masons need to make sure the bricks are lined up with each other.**

He also learned about cleaning and repairing broken masonry. Now, it was time to work with an experienced mason.

Logan would help work on the house. The house's owner wanted part of the house to have brick. Crews had already removed some of the house's wood siding. It sat in a large dumpster on the side of the house.

▲ **Only people who are trained should use saws.**

Logan's boss told him that his first task was to cut a few bricks with the brick saw. They had to be cut to fit what the wall needed. The mason showed Logan the blueprint. He pointed out how some of the bricks would need to be cut in half. He gave Logan the measurements. Logan used a measuring tape to carefully measure a brick. Then, he marked where the cut should be on the brick. The mason double checked the measurement.

They snapped on safety goggles, gloves, dust masks, and hearing protection before turning on the saw. The saw's motor roared when the mason turned it on. It was hooked up to a hose, and water dripped down the blade. Logan knew the water would help reduce the amount of dust from the sawed brick.

It would also help keep the saw blade cool. That helped prevent the blade from overheating, which can wear the blade out faster.

The mason slowly pushed the first brick into the blade. When the blade sliced through the heavy brick, there was a loud screeching noise. Then, the mason asked Logan if he would like to try. Logan grabbed a large red brick and cautiously slid it through the saw. He was careful to cut it at the right spot so it would fit perfectly on the house.

Then, the mason walked Logan over to the side of the house. It was a hot day. Sweat beaded on both of their foreheads. The mason showed Logan the plans for the brick wall. It would come halfway up the front of the house. The mason explained that it was very important that the brick be placed carefully. A wall should be straight, and it should not have bricks sticking out in odd places. It was also important to be careful with the mortar. The mortar would be mixed with water to make it easy to spread over the bricks. But too much water would cause the mortar to not be strong enough.

The mason explained that the mortar would be affected by the hot weather. The water in the mortar could **evaporate** in the heat. Then the mortar would not work as a glue with the bricks. Logan would have to work quickly to place the brick once the mortar was spread. But he still had to place the brick carefully.

▲ **Brick masons use trowels, a type of hand tool, to smooth mortar on bricks.**

Another mason had set down a straight line of bricks to start the wall. He gave Logan a tool called a trowel. It was like a spatula. Logan carefully dug some mortar out of a bucket. The mason told him to cover only four or five bricks at a time. That way the mortar would not dry out too fast before the next row could be placed. The trowel made a scratching noise as Logan set the mortar out. Then, he used the trowel to smooth the mortar down and make sure it was evenly spread out. Finally, the mason handed him a brick. Logan carefully put it down on the mortar and pressed it into place. He had finally started the work he had trained for.

CHAPTER FOUR

YEARS OF EXPERIENCE

It was early Monday morning and Juan got to the office before his staff. He owned a masonry company and wanted to look over the week's jobs. The morning air was cool and dew stuck to the green grass outside. But Juan knew it would get hot as the day went on. He would remind his employees to drink lots of water as they worked outside. Juan would also have his crew keep a close eye on a new apprentice that was starting this week. Juan needed to assign the apprentice some work.

There were many projects lined up for the week. The biggest one was work on a new grocery store. Juan also had customers who wanted brick patios and brick walls. One person needed to replace an old brick chimney. He looked at the schedule. He needed to decide where to send the apprentice first. Juan knew that the masons at his company were all good workers.

◄ **People with lots of experience can share their knowledge with others.**

▲ **Brick masonry is a physically demanding job.**

But he could not send the apprentice to just any job. It was better to start an apprentice with small jobs.

Masonry was hard work. Juan was often physically exhausted at the end of the day. A year earlier, he led a crew building a movie theater. It was very hot on several days. The brick masons got to work early. Sometimes, they got to work just as the sun was rising. That way they could work hard during the coolest part of the day. Juan remembered how sweaty his hands got inside his work gloves. It took many masons to put brick on the tall walls of the theater. All day long he heard the shouts of the masons as they worked.

▲ **Paying attention to detail is important for masonry work.**

It was different from working on a patio. A few weeks ago, Juan helped lay a large patio in a circle. Each brick had to be placed in exactly the right spot. If the crew wasn't careful, the brick circles would look messy. But they took their time and did it right. The homeowner thanked them and said it was beautiful.

Big jobs like the movie theater and difficult jobs like the patio were not beginner projects. Juan needed something else for the apprentice's first day. Then he remembered a customer who wanted a simple brick walkway in front of her house. Juan was confident the apprentice could successfully do that job with a team and learn while doing it.

▲ **Brick masons do their best to give clients what they want.**

Juan thought he might stop by and see how the grocery store project was going. It was a big project. He wanted to make sure nothing went wrong. He pulled up a copy of the store's blueprints on his computer. Paper blueprints had been used when he first started. Now, he could look at them online.

The blueprints had many details. They were created using different mathematical calculations. It was important to understand them. Someone who did not know how to read the plans could make errors. Those errors could cause the brick laying to go wrong.

Juan heard the sound of people coming into the office. The day was beginning for his masons. He shut his laptop and put it in his computer bag. He would stop at the grocery store project first. Then, he would visit the walkway where the apprentice would start. Juan would also check out an art museum. The museum wanted to know how much it would cost to build an outdoor patio and garden area made of brick. There were often new projects to work on as a brick mason, which kept the job interesting.

THINK ABOUT IT

► Why is it important that people specialize in different types of masonry work?
► What would the world around you look like without the work of brick masons?
► Why do so many people in trade jobs start out as apprentices?

GLOSSARY

apprenticeships (uh-PREN-tis-ships): Apprenticeships are a type of supervised work where someone learns trade skills. Some beginning brick masons work in apprenticeships.

blueprints (BLOO-prints): Blueprints are detailed plans of how something will be built. Brick masons might use blueprints to help build different structures.

concession (kuhn-SESH-uhn): A concession area is a business in a building where drinks and food are for sale. The concession stand sold hot dogs.

efficient (i-FISH-uhnt): Efficient means to not waste energy or time and to work well. Some buildings are made to be energy efficient.

evaporate (i-VAP-uh-rate): Evaporate means a liquid has changed into a gas or vapor. The water in brick mortar can evaporate on a hot day.

hydraulic (hye-DRAW-lik): Hydraulic machines are operated by the pressure of liquid. Brick masons often use hydraulic mixers to mix mortar.

mortar (MOR-tur): Mortar is a wet substance used to glue bricks together. Brick masons learn how to mix mortar under different conditions.

TO LEARN MORE

BOOKS

Cohn, Jessica. *On the Job in Construction*.
South Egremont, MA: Red Chair Press, 2017.

Kitts, W. L. *Great Jobs in the Skilled Trades*.
San Diego, CA: ReferencePoint Press, 2018.

Wilkinson, Colin. *Using Math in Construction*.
New York, NY: Rosen Central, 2018.

WEBSITES

Visit our website for links about brick laying: **childsworld.com/links**

Note to Parents, Teachers, and Librarians: We routinely verify our Web links to make sure they are safe and active sites. So encourage your readers to check them out!

SELECTED BIBLIOGRAPHY

Bryja, Jim. "Building with Structural Brick." *Mason Contractors Association of America*, 24 Sept. 2003, masoncontractors.org. Accessed 22 Mar. 2018.

"How to Build a Brick Veneer Wall." *Better Homes & Gardens*, 18 June 2018, bhg.com. Accessed 22 Mar. 2018.

"Masonry Workers." *Bureau of Labor Statistics*, n.d., bls.gov. Accessed 22 Mar. 2018.

INDEX

ABOUT THE AUTHOR

Amy C. Rea grew up in northern Minnesota and now lives in a Minneapolis suburb with her husband, two sons, and dog. She writes frequently about traveling around Minnesota.